NEW MEXICO

NEW MEXICO

MARCIA KEEGAN

Introduction by
HOWARD BRYAN

CLEAR LIGHT PUBLISHERS
SANTA FE, NM 87505

Dedicated to my husband and partner,
Harmon Houghton

CLEAR LIGHT PUBLISHERS
823 Don Diego, Santa Fe, New Mexico 87505
web site: www.clearlightbooks.com

© 1986 by Clear Light Publishers
Originally produced 1984 by Oxford
University Press (Canadian Branch)

ISBN 0-040666-02-0
10 9 8
Eighth Printing
Printed in Korea

INTRODUCTION

New Mexicans, believing that in New Mexico they possess a bit of paradise on earth, have lovingly dubbed their large but sparsely-populated state "The Land of Enchantment."

Realizing, however, that an overcrowded paradise can lose its enchantment, they are not averse to nourishing common misconceptions about the state that might tend to discourage mass immigration. Each person who moves to New Mexico wants to be the last to do so, assuming an attitude of "Now that I am here, let's close the door."

As a newcomer to New Mexico, more than fifty years ago, I entered upon the unfamiliar scene with certain misconceptions about the land, the climate and the people. Misconceptions, I might add, which remain prevalent today, and which have helped shape the long and often turbulent history of this vast, complex and misunderstood state.

Moving to New Mexico in 1948 from a Midwest industrial city I carried with me a mental picture of New Mexico as a flat desert, baked and parched the year around by a blazing sun, supporting little plant life other than sagebrush and cacti, and peopled to a large extent by Mexicans and Indians who didn't speak English. It was the lure of the frontier that drew me to my new home.

My false images quickly vanished as I became acquainted with my new surroundings and became aware of the history and culture of this bit of Indian and Hispanic America.

New Mexico has always been a land of myth and misconception, from the original myth of the Seven Cities of Cibola that lured the first European explorers to this inland region more than four centuries ago in a vain search for legendary cities that were believed to be made of gold. The Cibola myth lives on today in legendary stories of lost mines and buried treasures that lure modern adventurers to search the rugged landscape for instant wealth.

Myth and misconception contributed to New Mexico's relative obscurity as a remote part of the Spanish Empire, as a remote part of the Republic of Mexico and, for many years, as a remote part of the United States of America.

Always the myth of a barren and hostile land, often enforced again today in the minds of travelers on transcontinental highways and railroads that follow the easiest and least attractive paths through the state.

Even the name of the state projects a false image, causing surprising numbers of people in other parts of the United States and the world to confuse New Mexico with the Republic of Mexico, its neighbor to the south, or some other Latin American country, travel to which would require a passport or visa and a working knowledge of the Spanish language.

New Mexico students who apply for admission to East Coast universities receive such replies as, "We are not accepting any foreign students at this time." New Mexico housewives who order merchandise from Midwest mail order firms are sometimes told that, "We do not export goods out of the United States."

Still stranger is the fact that even some visitors to the state are not sure exactly where they are. No longer am I surprised when I hear tourists in Albuquerque, Santa Fe and Taos curio shops asking the clerks, "Do you accept American money?" or "Do you export goods to the United States?"

New Mexico, the state's official magazine, publishes a regular feature entitled "One Of Our Fifty Is Missing," in which New Mexicans relate amusing and sometimes frustrating experiences of being considered citizens of a foreign country.

Instances such as these inspired one journalist to suggest a new motto for the state: "New Mexico—The Nation's Best-Kept Secret."

Let me begin, then, by assuring you that New Mexico is a part of the United States, and has been since the Mexican War in 1846, when the United States, in its westward expansion, wrested this Southwest region away from Mexico. After more than sixty years as a US territory, New Mexico achieved full statehood in 1912 when it was officially admitted as the 47th state of the Union.

Although sparse in population, with little more than one million inhabitants, New Mexico ranks fifth among the fifty states in land area, with one and one-half million square miles. Strange, it seems, that such a large state could escape the notice of so many people.

Looking back on my arrival in New Mexico, I think the thing that surprised me most was the unanticipated diversity of land, diversity of climate and diversity of people.

Diversity of land might not have surprised me if I had known at the time that New Mexico's vast landscape ranges upward through six of the seven life zones found in North America, from the semi-tropical Sonoran Desert in the south to the above-timberline Alpine tundra of 13,000-foot mountain peaks in the north.

From Colorado to the north, the Rocky Mountains extend giant green fingers southward into north-central New Mexico, lofty ranges with softly-contoured peaks, covered with dense forests of pine, fir and spruce, concealing sparkling lakes and bubbling trout streams, inhabited by elk, deer, bear and mountain lions. No sooner do the mountains appear to die out than they suddenly spring up again to forested elevations in south-central and through western and southwestern areas of the state.

The brown foothills of the mountain ranges are dotted with small trees, piñon and juniper, these small and scattered trees extending up the slopes until they merge with the tall forests at rain- and snow-catching elevations.

From the eastern slopes of the easternmost mountains, the terrain gradually smooths out into treeless plains that extend to the Texas border and beyond. Only in the southeastern part of these plains, close to the Texas border, is one out of sight of the mountains.

Also from the Colorado Rockies comes the fabled Rio Grande, bisecting New Mexico from north to south, flowing swiftly through deep gorges at first and gradually slowing to a meandering river as it winds south through treacherous sandbars and quicksands, a sediment- and silt-carrying stream that often has a muddy appearance.

"A useless river," a visiting farmer once remarked, "too thick to drink, and too thin to plow."

But the Rio Grande creates a long and narrow oasis of green vegetation along its banks as it flows south through broad and semi-arid valleys, a fertile strip where irrigated farmlands produce fruits, vegetables, alfalfa and, near the southern border of the state, cotton.

During the late spring and early summer, the normally placid Rio Grande swells to a raging torrent as the northern mountains begin shedding their heavy blankets of winter snow, sending the water from melting snow gushing down the slopes to the river. A series of dams along the Rio Grande holds the floodwaters in check, at the same time creating large reservoirs that serve New Mexicans as water playgrounds in the desert.

After leaving New Mexico, the Rio Grande bends southeast to form the border of Texas and the Republic of Mexico as it completes its 1,885-mile journey from the Colorado Rockies to the Gulf of Mexico.

Much of New Mexico's landscape was shaped millions of years ago by widespread and tremendous volcanic eruptions, producing massive lava flows, accompanied by giant upheavals of earth. Evidences of this tumultuous period are quite apparent today in long-dormant volcanic craters, the tall and hardened necks of volcanic cones, hardened and now motionless lava flows, numerous hot springs that bubble to the surface, and slanted and twisted rock formations.

Among the most conspicuous features of the New Mexico landscape are the mesas, flat-topped hills that rise from the broad terrain, many having the appearance of pyramids with their top halves lopped off; and the arroyos, normally dry and sandy stream beds that carry water only after heavy rains in the vicinity.

Although much of New Mexico is high desert country, sparsely vegetated with a variety of small bushes, yucca plants and cacti, the closest thing I found to what I considered a true desert was the White Sands, in south-central New Mexico, a more than 200-square-mile expanse of pure white gypsum grains that roll and undulate into huge dunes as far as the eye can see, giving the broad valley a Sahara-like appearance. But, I was told, this is not a true desert, being instead a huge, natural pocket of gypsum.

In my early travels around the state I looked in vain for the giant saguaros, those tall cactus plants with uplifted arms that have come to symbolize the desert country of the American Southwest, only to learn that while they stand like silent sentinels on the low desert floors of southern Arizona, they do not extend eastward into New Mexico.

As for diversity of climate, I found that New Mexico, as much so as my native Midwest, has four separate and distinct seasons, each characterized by dramatic changes.

Spring is the least agreeable season of the year, a time of little rain, with strong afternoon winds often blowing clouds of sand and dust across the land, bringing complaints of "Enchantment blowing around" and "Arizona going by on its way to Texas." Summer brings blankets of wildflowers to the mountains, plains and deserts, and numerous thunderstorms that build up over the mountains and then drift off to drench selected areas of the land. Autumn chill is first felt by the aspen trees high in the mountain forests, their shimmering green leaves reacting by exploding into a brilliant yellow, the fall colors gradually spreading down to the river valleys in deep shades of red, gold and rust. Winter brings frequent snows to all parts of New Mexico, snow that evaporates quickly at lower elevations, but that blankets the mountains all winter and lingers into summer on the highest peaks.

Although one of the southern tier of states, New Mexico enjoys a cooler and much less humid climate than the others, due to its high and dry elevation. New Mexico's lowest elevation, 2,817 feet in the extreme southeast corner, is still higher than the highest elevations of seventeen other states.

Abundant winter sunshine brings mild temperatures in the afternoons, but winter nights can be bitterly cold, with temperature readings of 50 degrees below zero (Fahrenheit) not unknown in some mountain communities.

One of the first things I discovered about New Mexico's high altitude and resulting thin air is that it plays tricks on the body, bringing early fatigue, speeding inebriation, and causing optical illusions, such as making distant mountains appear to be within easy walking distance.

As for diversity of people, I found that New Mexicans had divided themselves into three major and distinct ethnic and cultural groups, American Indians, Spanish-Americans and Anglos, the word "Anglo" being used in New Mexico to identify almost anybody not of Indian or Spanish descent. In recent years, there has been a trend to refer to the Indians as Native Americans, and to the Spanish as Hispanics, Hispanos and Chicanos, but the Anglos are still called Anglos, despite the objections of a few of the many who are not of Anglo-Saxon descent.

The Indians, who make up about ten per cent of New Mexico's population, are again divided into three major tribal divisions, Pueblo, Navajo and Apache, with separate languages, customs and traditions.

The Pueblos, aboriginal inhabitants of the land, are so-called because for centuries they have lived sedentary lives in established towns or, to use the Spanish word, "pueblos." It is estimated that there were from sixty to seventy of these villages of mud and stone dotting the New Mexico landscape when the first Spanish explorers, led by Francisco Vasquez de Coronado, entered this region in AD 1540, but today there are nineteen scattered through northern and western parts of the state, on separate grants of land conferred by the Spanish Crown when Spain ruled New Mexico.

Pueblo origins are lost in the distant and misty past, but by the beginning of the fourteenth century they had already built and abandoned huge apartment dwellings of stone, some terraced to heights of four and five stories and containing enough rooms to accommodate more than 1,000 persons, the massive ruins of which still stand in solitude in the northwest part of the state. Most of the nineteen Indian pueblos of today date to about AD 1300, but one of them, Acoma, perched atop a 357-foot-high sandstone mesa in west-central New Mexico, is believed to be at least 1,000 years old and claims to be the oldest continuously-inhabited community in the United States.

Franciscan missionaries, who accompanied the earliest Spanish colonists to New Mexico, converted these Indians to Roman Catholicism in the seventeenth century, and the most conspicuous landmarks of their villages are the Franciscan mission churches, many of them centuries old. Less conspicuous, but just as important to the Indians, are the "kivas," secret chambers with rooftop entrances, where they still practice ancient rituals of their native religion and prepare for their periodic ceremonial dances, performed under a bright sun on the dusty plazas of the villages to the accompaniment of chanting and drumming.

Navajos and Apaches, nomads who began drifting south into New Mexico not long before the arrival of the Spaniards from the south, are now settled, for the most part, on reservation lands set aside for them by the United States government in the nineteenth century.

The Navajo lands are in the northwest quarter of the state, where many families live in scattered "hogans," octagonal, one-room dwellings that have much the appearance of large Eskimo igloos, except that instead of ice, they are made of logs or railroad ties chinked with earth. The once warlike Apaches, not subdued until the mid-1880s, occupy large tracts of mountain land in northern and south-central portions of the state.

Almost all Indians in New Mexico are bilingual, speaking English as well as their native tongues, and many are trilingual, speaking Spanish as well. Many earn their livelihood, or supplement their incomes, by the production and sale of exquisite (and expensive) native arts and crafts, including silver and turquoise jewelry, pottery and rugs.

The remainder of New Mexico's population is divided nearly equally between Hispanics and Anglos, the bilingual Hispanics speaking both Spanish and English fluently, most of the Anglo newcomers knowing only a few Spanish words and phrases.

Many New Mexico Hispanics claim descent from the first Spanish colonists who trudged north out of Mexico in 1598 under the leadership of Don Juan de Oñate, and who by 1610 had founded Santa Fe as New Mexico's capital, a decade before the Pilgrims landed at Plymouth Rock, 2,000 miles away on the East Coast. New Mexico remained a remote outpost of Spain's crumbling empire until 1821, when Mexico won its independence from Spain, and from 1821 to 1846 New Mexico was a remote outpost of the new Republic of Mexico.

Early civil and religious conflicts between Spanish authorities and the Pueblo Indians culminated in the great Pueblo Revolt of 1680, when the normally peaceful Pueblos, in a rare instance of determined unity, rose up and drove all the Spaniards out of New Mexico. Spain's rule over New Mexico was re-established in 1692-3, when Gen. Diego de Vargas and his Spanish conquistadores brought the rebellious Pueblos to submission in a series of military campaigns, and the Spanish colonists returned north to reoccupy their abandoned towns and haciendas.

It was the early Spaniards who brought to New Mexico the old Moorish custom of building with adobe bricks, bricks made of soft earth mixed with straw and dried to hardness in the hot sun. Earth-shaded adobe homes and buildings remain popular and appear as a natural part of the New Mexico landscape today.

Anglo newcomers (including some French-Canadian fur trappers) began drifting into New Mexico with the opening of the Santa Fe Trail from Missouri in 1821, their numbers sharply increasing when railroads penetrated the territory in the early 1880s, with the greatest immigration coming during the population boom that followed World War II.

Most Anglo-American newcomers, unaware of any particular cultural heritage of their own, have adopted the more attractive aspects of the cultures of their Hispanic and Indian neighbors.

They live in Pueblo and Spanish-styled adobe homes, brighten their living rooms with Navajo rugs and Mexican serapes, decorate their corner fireplace mantels with Indian pots and Hispanic woodcarvings, feast on chili-hot Mexican foods and, on Christmas Eve, outline their rooftops and sidewalks with hundreds of soft-glowing "luminaries," or "farolitos," an old Hispanic custom of placing lighted candles in a sand base inside upright brown paper sacks.

All New Mexicans have a strong sense of regional history, being surrounded on all sides by landmarks of history, from the 12,000-year-old camp sites of Stone Age hunters to a shallow depression in the desert where Los Alamos scientists detonated the world's first atomic bomb in 1945. On weekends and holidays, they follow uncrowded highways and byways of the state-to prehistoric Indian ruins, to the roofless walls of seventeenth century mission churches (abandoned a century before the more famous missions of California were founded), to deserted and crumbling nineteenth century mining towns and frontier military forts, and to Spanish fiestas and Indian ceremonial dances that celebrate past events and ancient traditions.

Among the prominent artists and writers from all over the world who sought and found escape in Santa Fe and Taos art colonies after the turn of the century was D.H. Lawrence, the troubled English novelist and poet, who lived and worked on three occasions in the early 1920s in the high Taos Valley of northern New Mexico, where his ashes are entombed today in a hillside chapel. In an essay entitled "New Mexico," Lawrence wrote: "I think New Mexico was the greatest experience from the outside world I have ever had. It certainly changed me for ever. Curious as it may sound, it was New Mexico that liberated me from the present era of civilization, the great era of material and mechanical development."

Lawrence might feel the same in New Mexico today.

During my nearly four decades in the state, I have seen but little change in New Mexico, except for centrally-located Albuquerque, the state's only major city, which has awkwardly absorbed most of the state's post-war population boom and now, with its immediate environs, bulges with nearly half the people living in New Mexico. But even here, urban din quickly gives way to mountain or desert solitude at the city limits, providing the city dwellers with quick escape from Lawrence's "era of material and mechanical development."

Many have felt the New Mexico mystique, but none more so than Marcia Keegan, who is unexcelled in capturing on color film the New Mexico imagery that produces in the beholder a feeling of spiritual enchantment. For twenty years she has wandered the length and breadth of the state, photographing with artistry and sensitivity the land and the people she loves. Over the years her color photographs of New Mexico have won her wide acclaim and have been published in many books, including her own, as well as in various periodicals.

Perhaps her color photographs, as displayed here, will help dispel some of the widely-held misconceptions about New Mexico. But then, there will be some New Mexicans who hope not.

HOWARD BRYAN

1 Pueblo dancers performing Ribbon Dance at night.

2 Ranch horses on a cattle range in northeastern New Mexico.

3 *(right)* White Sands National Monument, the world's largest gypsum desert.

4 *(left)* Sangre de Cristo Mountains near Santa Fe.

5 Adobe home and garden wall on Canyon Road in the heart of Santa
Fe's art colony. Dozens of galleries line the narrow street.

6 *(left)* Woman at watering hole, Acoma Pueblo.

7 The Garcia brothers in ceremonial attire at San Juan Pueblo.

8 *(left)* Tiny hilltop village of Los Ojos in northern New Mexico.

9 Autumn foliage of cottonwood trees on the banks of the Rio Grande.

10 San Ildefonso grandfather, Juan Cruz Roybal, and his grandchild, Bernice Roybal. San Ildefonso Pueblo is one of a number of New Mexico Indian pueblos bearing the names of Roman Catholic saints.

11 *(right)* Shiprock, towering landmark of the Navajo Reservation in northwestern New Mexico.

12 New Mexico religious folk art provides a colorful backdrop to an altar in the mission church at San Ildefonso Pueblo.

13 *(right)* The Green Corn Dance, San Ildefonso Pueblo.

14 Gila Cliff dwellings, in southwestern New Mexico, occupied by
prehistoric Indians in the 12th and 13th centuries.

15 Procession of Zuni Pueblo women carrying clay pots known as ollas on
their heads. They are known as Olla Women.

16 Hispanic art covers the walls of a small home in Santa Fe.

17 Low rider Arthur Medina of the Hispanic village of Chimayo. It is popular in Española and Chimayo for young men to fit hydraulic systems to
their cars which can suddenly lower the bodies down to a few inches off
the ground; these drivers call themselves "low riders."

18 *(left)* Leandro Bernal of Taos Pueblo displays a photo of himself.

19 View of the village of Lamy, near Santa Fe, on the Santa Fe Railway line.

20 Master potter Robert Tenerio from Santo Domingo Pueblo at work in his home.

21 *(right)* Natural outline of a bird on a sandstone cliff.

22 (*left*) The peaks of the rugged Sandia Mountains rise above Albuquerque to a height of 10,000 feet.

23 Apache Mountain Spirit Dancer at the annual Gallup Inter-Tribal Indian Ceremonial, where tribes from all over the country gather for festivities, dances, and arts and crafts.

24 Clayton Gibbard shoes a horse at Peñasco in northern New Mexico.

25 *(right)* The Rio Grande near Taos.

26 *(left)* Lights of Albuquerque at dusk, Sandia Mountains in distance.

27 Ceremonial dancers at San Ildefonso Pueblo.

28 "City of Rocks," the name given to an area of unusual rock formations
in southwestern New Mexico.

29 Ruins of an early 18th century Pecos Pueblo mission church. Pecos Pueblo was abandoned in 1838 and is now a national monument east of Santa Fe.

30 Double rainbow over Taos Pueblo.

31 *(right)* Cumbres & Toltec Scenic Railroad excursion train hauls summer sightseers along an old narrow-gauge line near the Colorado border.

32 Navajo artist R.C. Gorman in his Taos studio.

33 World-famous New Mexico mystery writer Tony Hillerman at his home in Albuquerque.

34 *(left)* Indian rodeo on the Mescalero Apache Reservation.

35 Miners once lived in these now abandoned frame houses in the old coal mining town of Madrid, now an arts community and tourist center.

36 Ruins of Pueblo Bonito in Chaco Canyon, abandoned since about 1130 AD. This huge, communal stone dwelling consisted of about 800 rooms and was terraced to four and five stories. It was built in the 11th century by ancestors of today's Pueblo Indians.

37 Comanche Dancers entering the Kiva at San Ildefonso Pueblo at the close of a ceremonial dance.

38 *(left)* Laguna Pueblo, in west
central New Mexico.

39 Indian girl of Acoma Pueblo.

40 *(left)* The world-famous Albuquerque International Balloon Fiesta is held each October in Albuquerque, "the balloon capital of the world." The event draws about a thousand hot-air balloons and around a million spectators from all over the world.

41 Waitress Thelma Chamberlin relaxes in a café in the old cowtown of Magdalena.

42 Some of the huge dish-shaped antennas at the Very Large Array (VLA) radio-telescope facility on the San Augustin Plains in west central New Mexico. the facility, operated by the National Radio Astronomy Observatory, detects radio waves and natural radiation in outer space.

There are 27 of thee antennas, each 82 feet in diameter and 92 feet high, which are moved about on a network of railroad tracks.

43 *(right)* Red rock country near Gallup.

44 Santa Fe resident Laura Wofford.

45 *(right)* Rural road in northern New Mexico.

46 Village of Alcalde, between Santa Fe and Taos.

47 Nambé Spear Dancer riding on his horse called Winter Hawk at Nambé Falls.

48 18th century mission church in the high mountain village of Las Trampas in northern New Mexico, a fine example of early Franciscan mission architecture.

49 *(right)* Sweet clover blankets a mountain prairie in northern New Mexico.

50 *(left)* Indian tribes from all over North America perform at the Gathering of Nations Pow Wow held annually in Albuquerque.

51 A cattle roundup near Chama in northern New Mexico.

52 Flowering cacti at White Oaks.

53 Rainbow over the Ortiz Hills south of Santa Fe.

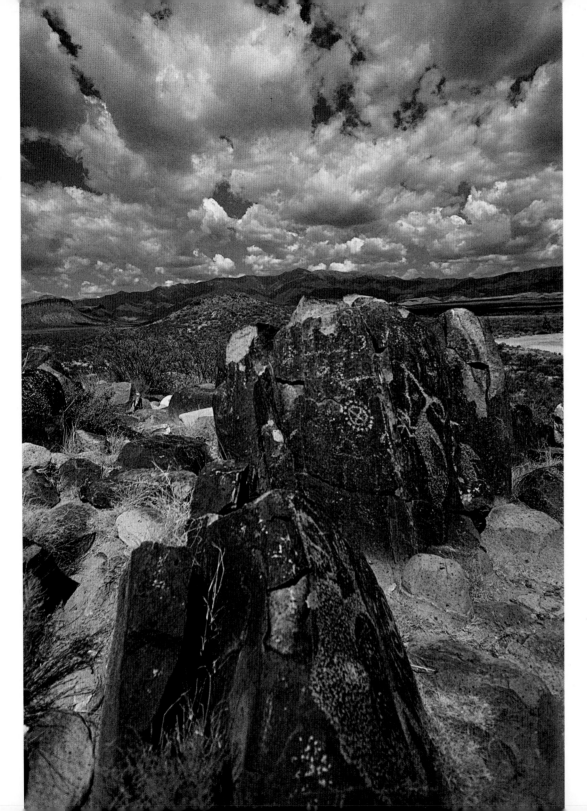

54　Petroglyphs (rock carvings) near Three Rivers in south central New Mexico; symbols and designs carved in the rocks by prehistoric Indians, dating back 10,000 years.

55　(*right*)　Forest lands in the mountains near Chama.

56 Ruins of Fort Union, on the Old Santa Fe Trail in northeastern New Mexico. This important military post was garrisoned by US troops from 1851 until abandoned in 1891.

57 *(right)* El Morro ("the bluff"), also known as Inscription Rock, in western New Mexico. The soft sandstone sides are covered with names and inscriptions carved into the rock by early travelers, the earliest having been carved in 1605 by Don Juan de Oñate, Spanish colonizer of New Mexico.

58 San Felipe Pueblo Casino Hollywood, north of Albuquerque.
Nine of the New Mexico Indian Pueblos operate casinos.

59 Winter scene in the valley below the "Atomic City" of Los Alamos.

60 Organ Mountains, east of Las Cruces in southern New Mexico.

61 Street scene in the village of Mesilla near the Mexican border.

62 *(left)* Multi-storied Taos Pueblo in the winter.

63 Indians of Tesuque Pueblo performing the Comanche Dance.

64 International Space Hall of Fame at Alamogordo, edge of the White Sands Missile Range.

65 *(right)* Prehistoric Indian pictograph (rock painting) near Silver City.

66 Montezuma Castle, United World College, USA, Montezuma. Originally built in the 1880s, it has been renovated and is an international center. Students come from around the world. The college combines intense academics with a spirit of international understanding.

67 *(right)* "Standing Rain," summer rainstorm on the mesa west of Albuquerque.

68 Newlyweds in a pickup truck near the old gold mining town of Golden.

69 *(right)* Windmill and water tank on a cattle ranch near Carrizozo in south central New Mexico.

70 *(left)* Veteran Santa Fe artist Tommy Macaione at work.

71 Sunflower near Silver City in southwest New Mexico.

72 *(left)* Boy polishing and selling cemetery monuments and statuary at Mesilla, near Las Cruces.

73 Small chapel in the village of Llanito near Las Vegas, the front decorated with contemporary Hispanic folk art.

74 Governor Gerald Nailor, who is also a famous artist, is restoring the mural in the church at Picuris Pueblo.

75 Rear view of the 18th Century Mission Church of St. Francis of Assisi
in Ranchos de Taos, showing the adobe buttresses.

76 *(left)* Sandstone rock formations at Ghost Ranch in northern New Mexico.

77 Moonrise over the mission church at Taos Pueblo.

78 Nestor Valdez in the old lumbering town of Chama in northern New Mexico.

79 *(right)* Old silver mining town of Cerrillos south of Santa Fe.

80 *(left)* Navajo Indian hogan, or family dwelling, near Thoreau in western New Mexico.

81 Lucy Martinez working on her pottery at San Ildefonso Pueblo.

82 A santo, or woodcarving of a
saint, an example of New Mexico
Hispanic religious folk art.

83 *(right)* Yvonne Lewis of Laguna
Pueblo with her daughter Tina.

84 *(left)* Anita Herrera, Las Vegas.

85 El Santuario de Chimayo, seen through handcarved wooden gates. This picturesque chapel was built in 1806 over sands believed to possess miraculous healing qualities. Now a Roman Catholic shrine, it attracts the ill and infirm who come to touch the sand, hoping to be healed. The Chapel is sometimes referred to as "the Lourdes of the Southwest."

86   Every September, the annual Fiesta de Santa Fe begins with the burning of Zozobra, or "Old Man Gloom." This fifty-foot high puppet is incinerated amidst an elaborate fireworks display to the delight of thousands of spectators.

87   *(right)* The historic San Felipe de Neri Roman Catholic Church in Albuquerque's Old Town, dating from 1706, is outlined with *luminarias*, also known as *faralitos*, on Christmas Eve. They are candles in upright brown paper sacks set in a sand base.

88 Rainbow near White Sands.